GOSCINNY AND UDERZO

PRESENT

An Asterix Adventure

ASTERIX AND THE PICTS

Written by JEAN-YVES FERRI
Illustrated by DIDIER CONRAD
Translated by ANTHEA BELL

Colour by THIERRY MÉBARKI, MURIELLE LEROI, RAPHAËL DELERUE

Congratulations to Jean-Yves Ferri and Didier Conrad for having the courage and talent to write and draw this new Asterix album. Thanks to them, the Gaulish village created with my friend René Goscinny can go on having new adventures to delight readers of the series.

Albert Uderzo

The memory of René Goscinny is never far away when Asterix is being brought to life. Until the present, the huge talent of Albert Uderzo has worked to preserve it. Today, now that Albert has watched over the production of the first album on which the original creators did not work, I like to think that my father would be proud of the authors to whom we have entrusted the famous little Gaul — as proud and happy as I am.

Anne Goscinny

FSC — MIX — Paper from responsible sources — FSC® C015829

Original edition © 2013 Les Éditions Albert René
English translation © 2013 Les Éditions Albert René
Original title: *Astérix chez les Pictes*

Exclusive licensee: Orion Publishing Group
Translator: Anthea Bell
Typography: Bryony Clark

The right of Jean-Yves Ferri to be identified as the author of this work and
the right of Didier Conrad to be identified as the illustrator of this work have been
asserted by them in accordance with the Copyright, Designs and Patents Act 1988.

First published in Great Britain in 2013 by
Orion Children's Books Ltd
Orion House
5 Upper St Martin's Lane
London WC2H 9EA
An Hachette UK company

1 3 5 7 9 10 8 6 4 2

Printed in Italy

www.asterix.com
www.orionbooks.co.uk

A CIP catalogue record for this book is available from the British Library

ISBN 978 1 4440 1167 8

The Orion Publishing Group's policy is to use papers that are natural, renewable and recyclable and made from wood grown in sustainable forests.
The logging and manufacturing processes are expected to conform to the environmental regulations of the country of origin.

BELGICA

GAULISH VILLAGE

COMPENDIUM

LAUDANUM

AQUARIUM

TOTORUM

ARMORICA

LUTETIA

GAUL
(ROMAN CONQUEST)
50 BC

CELTICA

AQUITANIA

PROVINCIA

THE YEAR IS 50 BC. GAUL IS ENTIRELY OCCUPIED BY THE
ROMANS. WELL, NOT ENTIRELY ... ONE SMALL VILLAGE OF
INDOMITABLE GAULS STILL HOLDS OUT AGAINST THE INVADERS.
AND LIFE IS NOT EASY FOR THE ROMAN LEGIONARIES WHO
GARRISON THE FORTIFIED CAMPS OF TOTORUM, AQUARIUM,
LAUDANUM AND COMPENDIUM ...

ASTERIX, THE HERO OF THESE ADVENTURES. A SHREWD, CUNNING LITTLE WARRIOR, ALL PERILOUS MISSIONS ARE IMMEDIATELY ENTRUSTED TO HIM. ASTERIX GETS HIS SUPERHUMAN STRENGTH FROM THE MAGIC POTION BREWED BY THE DRUID GETAFIX . . .

OBELIX, ASTERIX'S INSEPARABLE FRIEND. A MENHIR DELIVERY MAN BY TRADE, ADDICTED TO WILD BOAR. OBELIX IS ALWAYS READY TO DROP EVERYTHING AND GO OFF ON A NEW ADVENTURE WITH ASTERIX – SO LONG AS THERE'S WILD BOAR TO EAT, AND PLENTY OF FIGHTING. HIS CONSTANT COMPANION IS DOGMATIX, THE ONLY KNOWN CANINE ECOLOGIST, WHO HOWLS WITH DESPAIR WHEN A TREE IS CUT DOWN.

GETAFIX, THE VENERABLE VILLAGE DRUID, GATHERS MISTLETOE AND BREWS MAGIC POTIONS. HIS SPECIALITY IS THE POTION WHICH GIVES THE DRINKER SUPERHUMAN STRENGTH. BUT GETAFIX ALSO HAS OTHER RECIPES UP HIS SLEEVE . . .

CACOFONIX, THE BARD. OPINION IS DIVIDED AS TO HIS MUSICAL GIFTS. CACOFONIX THINKS HE'S A GENIUS. EVERY-ONE ELSE THINKS HE'S UNSPEAKABLE. BUT SO LONG AS HE DOESN'T SPEAK, LET ALONE SING, EVERYBODY LIKES HIM . . .

FINALLY, VITALSTATISTIX, THE CHIEF OF THE TRIBE. MAJESTIC, BRAVE AND HOT-TEMPERED, THE OLD WARRIOR IS RESPECTED BY HIS MEN AND FEARED BY HIS ENEMIES. VITALSTATISTIX HIMSELF HAS ONLY ONE FEAR, HE IS AFRAID THE SKY MAY FALL ON HIS HEAD TOMORROW. BUT AS HE ALWAYS SAYS, TOMORROW NEVER COMES.

OCCASIONALLY THE PLEASANT CLIMATE OF ARMORICA GAVE WAY TO THE STORMY WEATHER OF A HARD WINTER... IT SO HAPPENS THAT THIS MORNING, AFTER SEVERAL COLD DAYS, A PALE SUN COMES OUT AT LAST TO WARM THE LITTLE VILLAGE THAT WE KNOW SO WELL...

FRESH FISH! BUY MY NICE FRESH FISH!

UNHYGIENIX FISH SEAFOOD

HUH! FRESH, IS IT? TELL US ANOTHER!

HI, GERIATRIX! STILL A BIT NIPPY, EH?

OI! HERE'S CAESAR'S HEAD!

THAT WAS NOTHING TO SPEAK OF! I'VE SEEN WORSE!

IN THE YEAR 50 BV (BEFORE VITAL-STATISTIX), IT WAS SO COLD THAT THE SEA FROZE OVER! SEAGULLS CRASH-LANDED ON THE WAVES!

GERIATRIX, WHAT ARE YOU DOING OUT IN THIS WEATHER? YOU KNOW YOU'LL CATCH YOUR DEATH!

...FROZEN SEA MONSTERS CAME UP FROM THE SEA!

WE PUSHED THEM BACK WITH STALACTITES.

POOR OLD GERIATRIX! HE'S ALWAYS BEEN INCLINED TO RAMBLE ON.

18

5

ASTERIX, DO YOU REALLY THINK THERE'S TOO MUCH SNOW TO GO HUNTING WILD BOAR?

YES, OBELIX. BUT WE CAN ALWAYS LOOK FOR OYSTERS.

YOU'RE RIGHT, IT'S FEBRUARY.

AND FEBRUARY IS A MONTH WITH AN "R" IN IT!

FEBRUARY EVEN HAS TWO "R"S IN IT.

SO THE WORLD'S OUR OYSTER!

I LOVE WALKING ON THE BEACH AFTER A STORM, FINDING ALL THE THINGS CAST UP BY THE SEA.

LOOK AT THAT, ASTERIX!

2A

A DENTED OLD HELMET, JUST THE THING FOR MY COLLECTION!

AND AN OLD AMPHORA!

GREEK OR PHOENICIAN, I'M NOT SURE WHICH...

AND A BLOCK OF ICE, ASTERIX. CAN IT REALLY BE A BLOCK OF ICE?

GRR

OF COURSE, OBELIX. REMEMBER WHAT GERIATRIX SAID!

GRR

YES... BUT A BLOCK OF ICE WITH SOMEONE INSIDE IT LOOKING OUT AT ME?

WOOF! WOOF!

!

2B

NO, OBELIX, THERE'S NO DOUBT ABOUT IT, WE HAVE HERE A PICT FROM DISTANT CALEDONIA!*

* SCOTLAND

A WHAT?

A PICT!

DON'T JUST STAND THERE, BOYS! WHEN YOU'VE PICKED UP THE PICT TAKE HIM TO GETAFIX'S HUT.

YES, QUIIIICK!

HE'S SLIIIPPP-ERY...

WHO IS?

THIS PICT!

WHAT CAN HAVE HAPPENED TO HIM, O DRUID?

WHO KNOWS, VITALSTATISTIX?

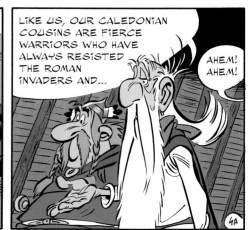

LIKE US, OUR CALEDONIAN COUSINS ARE FIERCE WARRIORS WHO HAVE ALWAYS RESISTED THE ROMAN INVADERS AND...

AHEM! AHEM!

SO SORRY TO INVADE YOU LIKE THIS.

LET ME INTRODUCE MYSELF: LIMITEDNUMBUS, HERE TO TAKE A CENSUS.

MY COLLEAGUES AND I ARE TRAVELLING THE MOST REMOTE PROVINCES TO COUNT THE POPULATION AND DRAW UP A LIST OF THEIR ACTIVITIES.

ER... IS THERE A PROBLEM? AM I INTERRUPTING A TRADITIONAL CEREMONY?

BUT DON'T WORRY! THIS IS A PURELY ADMINISTRATIVE INQUIRY. ITS SOLE AIM IS TO SLIM DOWN THE FAT CATS AMONG THE LOCAL...

I'LL SHOW YOU WHO'S A FAT CAT!

STOP IT, OBELIX! THIS LITTLE CLERK IS ONLY OBEYING ORDERS.

I CAN CONFIIIRM THAT! ANYWAY, I'M FAMOUS FOR MY LACK OF INITIATIVE!

RIGHT, YOU CAN TAKE YOUR CENSUS, ROMAN, BUT GET ON WITH IT QUICKLY AND BE DISCREET.

YOUR (GULP) REQUEST HAS BEEN RECORDED.

NOW, EVERYONE OUT, AND LET'S LEAVE OUR DRUID TO WATCH OVER THE CASTAWAY.

5A

NO, NO! I'M GOING HOME ON FOOT. TOO MUCH BLACK ICE ABOUT!

ARE YOU SURE YOU WOULDN'T RATHER STAY IN A GROUP TO HAVE THE CENSUS TAKEN?

YOU JUST WAIT, THEY'LL COME IN THEIR THOUSANDS, ALL IN BLOCKS OF ICE!

CALM DOWN, GERIATRIX POPPET!

POOR BOY! SO YOUNG! I DO HOPE HE GETS OVER IT!

AND SO ELEGANT! DID YOU SEE THOSE TRENDY TATTOOS?

AND THAT EXOTIC LITTLE KILT!

I MUST SAY, IT'S A CHANGE FROM OUR OAFISH GAULISH MENFOLK WITH THEIR BIG CONKS!

TEEHEEHEE! YOU'RE RIGHT, BACTERIA.

PFFR!

5B

SEVERAL HOURS LATER.

AND NOW TO STIMULATE THE PULSE GENTLY.

HAWTHORN LEAF, MISTLETOE LEAVES, CAMOMILE OIL...

TINK!

HE MUSTN'T COME ROUND TOO SUDDENLY.

NOW WHAT DID I DO WITH MY POT OF CAMOMILE OIL?

THAT'LL TEACH ME TO LABEL MY POTS!

6A

...XIV, XV.

HEY! JUST A MOMENT, PLEASE. IT'S FOR THE CENSUS.

SURNAME, FIRST NAME, PROFESSION. PERMANENT OR TEMPORARY RESIDENT?

CRK.

HOW DO YOU SPELL THAT?

CRK

6B

COME QUICK! THE PICT HAS ESCAPED!

PICKING UP THE TRAIL OF A PICT IS A PICKY BUSINESS, RIGHT, ASTERIX?

AT LEAST IT PROVES THAT HE'S FEELING BETTER.

I CAN CONFIRM THAT!

SSH! HE'S TELLING HIS STORY.

FOUR!

STORMS?

WHIRLWINDS?

MUSHROOMS?

FAR AWAY!

SOME-WHERE ELSE!

NEAR COMPENDIUM!

VICTORY!

REJOICING!

STERNUM!

ER...

LET'S SEE...

WE'LL GO OVER IT AGAIN...

I GET IT! A TERRIBLE STORY! HE WAS EATING MUSHROOMS AT FOUR ON THE DOT WHEN A WHIRLWIND HIT HIM RIGHT IN THE STOMACH.

NEVER MIND THE DETAILS OF YOUR DESPERATE BATTLES AGAINST THE ROMANS, O PICT!

FROM NOW ON OUR HOME IS YOURS! LET ME TELL YOU, TO US GAULS THE RIGHT OF ASYLUM REALLY MEANS SOMETHING!

HUH! YOU AND YOUR FINE SPEECHES!

CAN'T YOU SEE IN HIS EYES THAT HE'S TELLING US A TRAGIC LOVE STORY?

SHOW US WHAT YOU'RE HIDING IN YOUR LITTLE CLENCHED FIST, O PICT!

OOOOH! IMPEDIMENTA IS RIGHT!

A GOLD RING!

IS THAT PART OF THE MIME?

OH, HOW LOVELY! OH, HOW SWEET!

A REAL NORDIC SAGA!

MAYBE, BUT WHAT'S IT GOT TO DO WITH MUSHROOMS?

WATCH OUT! HE'S FREEZING UP AGAIN!

QUICK, TAKE HIM TO THE DRUID!

NO! STAY IN A GROUP!

BUT... BUT WHAT ABOUT MY SPEECH?

WE'VE FOUND HIM, GETA-FIX!

YOU DON'T SAY! I WAS SURE IT WAS OVER THERE.

12

A SENSE OF SOLIDARITY SOON DEVELOPS IN THE VILLAGE...

I'VE MADE HIM A NICE CAKE!

I'VE BROUGHT SOME REALLY FRESH FISH.

AND HERE ARE TOOLS TO CUT HIS CHAINS.

AREN'T YOU GIVING ME ANY OF THAT CAKE, IMPEDIMENTA?

YOU'RE FAT ENOUGH AS IT IS!

IF YOU ASK ME, IMPEDIMENTA, YOU'RE PAYING TOO MUCH ATTENTION TO THAT PICT.

MAYBE. HE REMINDS ME VAGUELY OF SOMEONE.

WHAT DO YOU MEAN, THE PICT REMINDS YOU OF SOMEONE?

HE REMINDS ME OF A RED-HEADED YOUNG WARRIOR, LONG AGO, WHO MADE ME DREAM.

POF POF POF

RED-HEADED YOUNG WARRIOR? WHAT RED-HEADED YOUNG WARRIOR?

I DON'T KNOW NOW... HE WASN'T SO FAT THEN.

9A

???

THEY'RE ALL THE SAME, IMPEDIMENTA DEAR! MINE THINKS OF NOTHING BUT FISH!

AND APART FROM HAMMERING ON HIS ANVIL, MINE...

SO YOU'RE PATHETIX, ARE YOU, CHIEF?

LOOKS LIKE IT.

MEANWHILE...

HE KEEPS LOOKING SADLY AT HIS RING, GETAFIX.

DO YOU WANT TO GO BACK TO THE LAND OF THE PICTS, COUSIN?

HE CAN'T TELL YOU, OBELIX. HE'S LOST HIS VOICE.

DRINK THIS ELIXIR, O PICT.

SMELLS GOOD. CAN I HAVE SOME?

9B

BUT AT NIGHTFALL...

POOR MAN, HE DOESN'T KNOW WHERE HE IS. HE'S GETTING A FIX ON THE STARS...

WE MUST HELP HIM TO RETURN TO HIS VILLAGE, GETAFIX!

I KNOW, ASTERIX. I'M AFRAID FOR THAT HE'D HAVE TO BE ABLE TO TELL US WHERE HE COMES FROM.

IS THE LAND OF THE PICTS AS HIGH UP AS THAT?

NEXT DAY...

AND WHEN NIGHT COMES, HE LOOKS SADLY AT THE STARS!

ISN'T THAT JUST LOVELY?

HE'S SIGHING FOR THE GIRL HE LOVES, THAT'S FOR SURE!

I'VE HAD ENOUGH OF THIS! OUR WIVES HAVE EYES ONLY FOR THAT PICT!

PICT AND CHOSEN BY EVERY LAST ONE OF THEM!

THEY'VE ALL PEEKED AT HIM, DON'T ASK ME WHY!

LET'S COMPLAIN TO THE CHIEF!

OH, GOOD, GENTLEMEN! I WANT YOU TO HELP ME PLUMB THE DEPTHS OF YOUR SOCIETY!

MMMBL

NOW THEN, LADS, CALM DOWN! AS YOU KNOW, WE OWE OUR GUEST THE RIGHT OF ASYLUM, AND...

SPEAKING OF ASYLUMS, AM I IN A LOONY BIN?

MY FEVER PASSES OFF, AND I'M DRESSED LIKE THIS! IS IT THE LATEST FASHION, OR WHAT?

HELLO, BOYS! DO YOU LIKE IT?

BECAUSE THERE'S PLENTY OF FABRIC LEFT TO MAKE YOU ALL NEW BREECHES!

NO, NO! THIS TIME THEY'VE GONE TOO FAR WITH THEIR PICT!

THEIR WHAT?

AT ONCE...

GETAFIX, THIS IS SERIOUS! WE HAVE TO TALK ABOUT YOUR PICTISH FRIEND!

...AND AFTER SOME EMBARRASSED EXPLANATIONS...

IN SHORT – HOW CAN I PUT IT? – HIS POPULARITY WITH THE VILLAGE WOMEN, ER...

...CALLS THE RIGHT TO ASYLUM INTO QUESTION, IS THAT IT?

ASTERIX! GETAFIX! QUICK! COME AND LOOK!

12A

I WAS JUST SHOWING HIM MY MENHIRS. IT DOES AN INVALID GOOD TO LOOK AT MENHIRS...

OBELIX QUARRY CAREFUL MENHIRS TURNING

...AND THEN HE PICKED UP MY TOOLS AND HE DID **THAT!**

MY WORD! I'D SWEAR IT'S NORTHERN CALEDONIA!

AND SEE THAT CROSS?

BUT THEN... IF HE REMEMBERS WHERE HE LIVES...

IN THAT CASE...

WE CAN TAKE HIM BACK TO **THE LAND OF THE PICTS,** BY TOUTATIS!

OH, YE'LL TAKE THE HIGH ROAD

WOOF!

12B

16

AND SO, ONE FINE SPRING DAY, IT IS TIME TO LEAVE...

NO, OBELIX! IT'S NOT WORTH THE TROUBLE OF TAKING THAT MENHIR WITH US!

ASTERIX, I'M GIVING YOU SOME MAGIC POTION AND A GOURD OF THIS ELIXIR FOR OUR PICTISH FRIEND. ONE SPOONFUL MORNING AND EVENING.

I UNDERSTAND, O DRUID.

DOGMATIX IS RATHER SMALL FOR SUCH A LONG VOYAGE. I'LL LEAVE HIM WITH YOU, GETAFIX. ONE BONE MORNING AND EVENING.

AND I TELL YOU I LOOK RIDICULOUS DRESSED LIKE THIS!

NOT AT ALL, THE EFFECT IS SLIMMING! AND YOU CAN SEE THAT IT GIVES OUR GUEST PLEASURE.

13A

I KNOW IT'S SILLY, BUT I'VE NEVER LIKED MY KNEES.

AND WHEN I CATCH A COLD IT ALWAYS STARTS IN MY FEET.

DON'T LISTEN, GERIATRIX SWEETIE-PIE! EVERYTHING SUITS YOU!

SMACK!

NOW TO BRING MY CENSUS UP TO DATE: MINUS THREE WARRIORS, PLUS ONE DOG... I WISH THESE GAULS WOULDN'T KEEP MOVING ALL THE TIME!

WAIT! WAIT! I'VE COMPOSED A CALEDONIAN TWO-STEP FOR THEIR DEPARTURE!

POC!

SPLASH!

WHAT HAPPENED?

HE MISSED A STEP AGAIN.

13B

17

I WAS LEADING A PEACEFUL LIFE WITH MY CLAN, NEAR THE CLEAR WATERS OF LOCH ANDROLL...

...WHEN I FELL INTO AN AMBUSH SET BY THE ODIOUS MACCA-BAEUS.

MACCA-BAEUS?

THE CHIEFTAIN OF THE MACCABEES CLAN ON THE OPPOSITE BANK. HE HAD ME TIED TO A TREE TRUNK AND THROWN INTO THE WATER. IT'S CALLED TOSSING THE CABER.

WHY DID HE DO THAT, O PICT?

THAT WRETCH WANTED CAMOMILLA, THE ADOPTED DAUGHTER OF OUR LATE KING THE GOOD MAC II, FOR HIMSELF!

CAMOMILLA, MY LOVELY FIANCÉE, WHOSE DIAPHANOUS BEAUTY MAKES THE SPARKLING WATERS OF THE LOCH LOOK MURKY...

EEEURGH!!

'SCUSE ME, BUT SOPPY LOVE STORIES CHURN ME UP!

⑮A

LISTEN, I DIDN'T UNDERSTAND ALL THAT! COULD YOU BEGIN AGAIN AT THE BEGINNING, COUSIN?

OOO...

PERSONALLY I'D RATHER HAVE A QUICK SUMMARY, IF IT'S ALL THE SAME TO YOU...

AND THE CROSSING CONTINUES...

IF YOU WANT TO UNDERSTAND MY COUNTRY, I MUST MENTION OUR CLANS, WHICH HAVE BEEN DIVIDED SINCE THE DEATH OF KING MAC II. IT'S PERFECTLY SIMPLE...

THERE ARE THE EASTERN PICTS AND THE WESTERN PICTS, THE SEA-GOING PICTS WHO PAINT THEMSELVES GREEN, AND THE BLUE PICTS WHO ARE FLESH-COLOURED. THEN THERE ARE THE BROWN PICTS, THE TWO-TONE PICTS...

I THINK I PREFERRED IT WHEN HE'D LOST HIS VOICE.

⑮B

19

AT THE SAME TIME, FURTHER NORTH ON A REMOTE PART OF THE COAST...

SO THIS IS THE FAMOUS LAND OF THE PICTS, FALLACIUS...

CAREFUL, PRETENTIUS! IN GENERAL THOSE BARBARIANS LEAVE US BRUISED IN ALL THE COLOURS OF THE RAINBOW.

YOU'RE RIGHT. ACCORDING TO OUR EMISSARIES, IT'S EASY TO GET STUCK IN THIS MARSHY TERRAIN...

ASK THAT SHEPHERD OVER THERE THE WAY.

THE MACCABEES CLAN? EASY! THEY'RE RED... EACH CLAN HAS ITS OWN COLOUR.

16A

NOT A BAD IDEA. AND WHAT DO YOU CALL THESE, PICT?

PICTOGRAMS.

WHAT DOES THAT ONE OVER THERE SAY?

ROAD LIABLE TO FLOODING.

OH. IS IT SAFE?

FAIRLY SAFE.

?

COME ON, THEN. LET'S GET OUT OF THIS QUAGMIRE AND CARRY ON, BY JUPITER.

16B

MEANWHILE...

AND HERE IS LOCH ANDROLL! HOW DELIGHTFUL TO HEAR THE SCARLET GROUSE AND THE MELODIOUS SONG OF THE MACPUFFIN AGAIN!

WILL CAMOMILLA HAVE FORGOTTEN ME? OH, BY GREAT NESSIE! WHO KNOWS HOW MUCH TIME HAS PASSED SINCE I LEFT?

HE TALKS ALL THE TIME, ASTERIX. IS THAT NORMAL?

PROBABLY A SIDE-EFFECT OF THE ELIXIR.

WHO IS THIS NESSIE YOU SPEAK OF, MACAROON?

THE GUARDIAN OF THE LOCH AND OUR TOTEM ANIMAL, ASTERIX.

MIND-YOUR-OWN-BUSINESS IN FULL. SHE COMES AND GOES AS SHE LIKES, AND DRIVES THE SALMON INTO MY CLAN'S NETS.

I SEE.

A KIND OF OTTER.

21

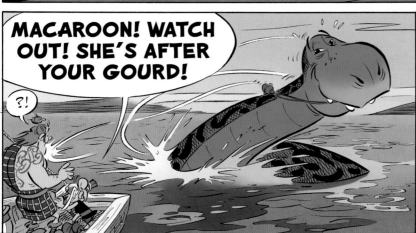

* CELTIC GODDESS OF THE UNDERWORLD

* GOD OF NOISE AND BEES

19A

19B

23

JUST LOOK AT THEIR ROAD SIGNS! THEY'RE FUNNY!

AND USEFUL IN THE FOG!

WHAT DOES THAT ONE MEAN?

WE CALL IT A ROUNDABOUT. IT LEADS ANY PURSUERS ASTRAY.

AT THE SAME MOMENT...

SINCE WHEN DID THE DEAD COME BACK TO LIFE?

THAT'S ENOUGH SUPERSTITIOUS TALK! WHAT WILL OUR ROMAN ALLIES THINK? THEY'RE BANG UP TO DATE WITH THE VERY LATEST IN THE ANCIENT WORLD!

BUT IT REALLY IS HIM, O MACCABAEUS! THE GHOST OF MACAROON ON THE OPPOSITE BANK!

...ESCORTED BY TWO EMISSARIES FROM THE OTHER WORLD IN SUPERNATURAL CLOTHING!

ONE OF THEM, THE FAT ONE, WORE A FUNNY TARTAN...

...NOT SQUARES, A SORT OF STRIPED PATTERN!

SORT OF... STRIPED?

ONLY BEINGS FROM ANOTHER WORLD COULD WEAR SUCH HORRIBLE BREECHES!

HMM, ER... ALL RIGHT! ANYWAY, SEE WHAT'S GOING ON OPPOSITE AND REPORT BACK TO ME.

AT THE SAME TIME...

AND HERE IS MY VILLAGE!

KROKA KROKA KROKA

WELL?

CAN'T I GIVE OUR OWN RALLYING CRY?

21A

HELLO... PEOPLE ARE REPLYING!

I'D CALL IT MORE OF A WHISTLING...

?!

SLAM

AHA! FEAR NOTHING! IT'S JUST A LITTLE GAME POPULAR IN THESE PARTS, CALLED TOSSING THE CABER!

CAN I PLAY TOO? CAN I PLAY TOO?

21B

OBELIX, NOOOOOOOO!

AS USUAL, MISTER OBELIX CHARGES ON WITHOUT THINKING!

AND AS USUAL, MISTER ASTERIX SEES THE STRAW IN HIS NEIGHBOUR'S EYE!

WHICH OF YOU IS HAVING FUN THROWING CABERS?

MACAROON? MAY THE GREAT THISTLE PRICK ME! IS IT REALLY YOU?

MACMINI, MY LITTLE BROTHER! NO?! — HIP HOP — I'M DREAMING! THIS IS IMPOSSIBLE!

BY GREAT NESSIE, IT'S TOO CRUEL! ALL IS CLEAR NOW!

?

I'VE SPENT YEARS AND YEARS IN THE ICE, AND MY LITTLE BROTHER IS AN OLD MAN!

?

NO, NO, YOU'VE GOT THE WRONG END OF THE CABER. I'M YOUR GREAT-UNCLE MACLAREN, AND HERE'S MACMINI!

HI, LITTLE BROTHER!

OUR DRUID FORETOLD YOUR RETURN!

?

KRRRRR

IT'S A MIRACLE!

LET'S GO AND TELL THE WHOLE VILLAGE!

KROKA KROKA KROKA

WAIT! WAIT! SEE MY RALLYING CRY! IT WORKS!

YES, YES! THAT'LL DO, OBELIX. COME ON!

AND OUR FRIENDS ENTER THE PICTISH VILLAGE IN TRIUMPH...

BLEAT BLEAT BLEAT

MACMAMA! MACROCOSM! MACADAMIA! CATALPA! ARNICA! MACROBIOTIX OUR DRUID! HOW GOOD TO SEE YOU ALL AGAIN!

BLEAT BLEAT

COUSINS, LET ME INTRODUCE MY FAMILY. IT'S VERY SIMPLE: WE MAKE UP ONE BIG CLAN!

MACLAREN IS THE UNCLE BY MARRIAGE OF CATALPA, THE ADOPTED NIECE OF MACMAMA, WHO IS THE SECOND WIFE OF THAT NUTCASE MACADAMIA, MY STEPFATHER, WHO IS ALSO GODFATHER TO ARNICA, MY LITTLE COUSIN ON THE REAL MACCOY SIDE OF THE FAMILY...

SCRATCH SCRATCH

MANY A MACKLE MAKES A MUCKLE...

23A

THAT'S ENOUGH TALKING! YOU MUST BE WORN OUT. EVERYONE COME AND HAVE A NICE HOT MEAL!

THAT MAKES SENSE!

THREE CHEERS FOR MACMAMA!

I'M GOING TO LIKE IT HERE!

I FEEL SO HAPPY – I JUST HAVE TO TOSS A CABER!

OBELIX! NOOOO!!!

BLEAT

I DON'T LIKE THIS MISSION... IT'S TOO CALM. I HAVE A NASTY FEELING.

THAT'S FUNNY, I HAVE A KIND OF WHISTLING IN MY EARS...

23B

27

OBELIX, OLD FRIEND, YOU'LL END UP HURTING SOMEONE!

OH, YES? SO MISTER ASTERIX DOESN'T APPROVE OF HIGHLAND GAMES, IS THAT RIGHT?

COLLIDING WITH A TREE IN THE MIDDLE OF THE FOG! IT'S NOT NATURAL!

THAT'S IT! WE'RE TURNING BACK. WE'LL SAY WE COULDN'T SEE THE WAY.

MEANWHILE, ON THE OTHER SIDE OF THE LOCH, THE ROMANS ARE MAKING PROGRESS...

NEARLY THERE, FALLACIUS. I'LL SPEAK TO THE MEN.

LEGIONARIES!
LET ME REMIND YOU, WE ARE ON AN ULTRA-SECRET MISSION IN PICTISH TERRITORY!

24A

WHAT? SPEAK UP, WE CAN'T HEAR YOU HERE AT THE BACK!

WE ARE HERE AT THE INVITATION OF CHIEF MACCABAEUS, A FAR-SIGHTED CHIEFTAIN WHO WANTS AN ALLIANCE WITH ROME!

HOME SWEET HOME. I NEVER DID LIKE ROAMING.

AND SO, MEN, I EXPECT AN EXEMPLARY ATTITUDE FROM YOU. OUR PASSWORD IS COURAGE AND BRAVERY!

OFF WE GO!

PORRIDGE AND GRAVY? THAT SOUNDS A BIT OF ALL RIGHT. WHAT DO YOU SAY, LADS?

24B

THE FAMILY PARTY FOR THE RETURN OF MACAROON IS IN FULL SWING...

THIS IS VERY GOOD, MACMAMA. WHAT IS IT?

SALMON PARCELS. AND THEN THERE'LL BE MACKEREL WITH MACARONI.

SO I MANAGED TO GET ONE HAND FREE, BUT THE CURRENTS KEPT TAKING ME FURTHER NORTH...

MACAMA... COMACA... COMRADES!

HUSH! LISTEN!

IT'S OUR DRUID SPEAKING.

DIDN'T I TELL YOU MACAROON WOULD BE BACK? REMEMBER? HIC! I HAD A VISION IN THE...

THE MALTED WATER OF LIFE!

YES. VERY TRUE.

MACRO-BIOTIX DID SAY SO!

I SAW A BLOCK OF ICE... HIC! AN ENORMOUS BLOCK OF ICE, FLOATING.

MALTED WATER?

IT'S OUR NATIONAL DRINK, MADE OF FERMENTED MALT. THE WATER OF LIFE. IT'S VERY STRONG!

THANKS TO IT, I SURVIVED IN THE ICE. WE DRINK IT WITH PLENTY OF ADDED WATER, BUT THE MACCABEES DRINK IMMODERATELY.

OUIIIIIIIIIY

BOOM BOOM TINGALING, TINGALONG.

HUSHABYE BABY ON THE TREE TOP, WHEN THE WIND BLOWS YOU'LL FALL IN THE LOCH

AH, A LOCH ANDROLL TUNE PLAYED BY OUR BARDS!

CLACK CLACK CLACK CLACK CLACK

ALL THIS NOISE DURING A MEAL... IT CAN'T BE A GOOD IDEA!

OBELIX!

THINK BEFORE YOU HIT ANYONE. THESE PEOPLE MAY RESPECT THEIR BARDS MORE THAN WE RESPECT OURS.

YOU THINK SO?

YES... HERE THEY USUALLY JUST CLAP THEIR HANDS.

AH! YOU SEE?

29

AT THE SAME MOMENT, ON THE OPPOSITE BANK...

MACCABAEUS, FUTURE KING OF THE PICTS, WELCOMES HIS ROMAN ALLIES!

AVE MACCABAEUS. THROUGH US, JULIUS CAESAR'S VANGUARD SALUTES YOU!

PORRIDGE AND GRAVY!

WHAT'S WRONG? WEREN'T WE SUPPOSED TO GIVE THE PASSWORD?

27A

YOU'RE JUST IN TIME FOR THE CEREMONY, O ROMAN!

NO PROBLEMS – THE WAY WAS WELL SIGNPOSTED.

COME ON UP AND I'LL TELL YOU MY PLANS!

NOT YOU, YOU IDIOTS. YOU STAY HERE AND FRATERNISE WITH OUR ALLIES.

ER... AVE!

HOW'S TRICKS?

THE TIMES ARE OUT OF JOINT, AS YOU MIGHT SAY.

THAT'S RIGHT...

AND IS THAT YOUR NATURAL COLOUR?

27B

SUPPOSE WE TOSSED SOME CABERS AT THEM?

IT WON'T WORK, OBELIX. THE VILLAGE OF THE MACCA-BEES IS VERY STRONG, AND THEIR CLIFF IS AS FULL OF HOLES AS A HELVETIAN CHEESE. THEY TAKE REFUGE THERE AT ANY ALARM.

I'M NOT SURPRISED! HE'S SMALL ANYWAY, AND HE SPOKE UP SO LATE.

HE'S PALE. IT MUST BE HIS LIVER!

IN THAT CASE WE HAVE NO CHOICE! WHERE WILL THE CEREMONY TAKE PLACE?

ON THE ISLAND IN THE MIDDLE OF THE LOCH. WHOEVER CLAIMS THE THRONE MUST ACCEPT THE ACCLAMATION OF ALL THE OTHER CLAN CHIEFTAINS.

LISTEN, THEN, MACAROON! TOMORROW YOU WILL SPEAK UP IN FRONT OF THE ASSEMBLY AND CONFUSE MACCABAEUS.

CONFUSE HIM... HIC! WHO WITH?

YOU... YOU'RE RIGHT, ASTERIX! I WILL STAND BEFORE HIM, AND I'LL SAY... I'LL...

I'LL TELL HIM... I... 'TWAS BRILLIG, AND THE SLITHY TOVES...

BY BUG!* HE'S GOING OFF THE RAILS AGAIN.

IT'S A DISASTER!

HE'S RELAPSING!

* BUG: GOD OF VIRUSES AND OATHS.

HE NEEDS GETAFIX'S ELIXIR TO RESTORE HIS VOICE. BUT THEIR MONSTER HAS CARRIED OFF THE GOURD.

OH YES! THE BIG OTTER!

COME ON! TELL HIM, MACMINI!

I KNOW! NESSIE HIDES EVERYTHING SHE FINDS IN HER CAVE ON THE EDGE OF THE LOCH. I CAN TAKE YOU THERE IF YOU LIKE.

AT NIGHT-FALL...

I DRANK – *HIC!* – THERE'LL BE FOUR OF THEM, COMING FROM GAUL TO HELP US!

WE'LL LOOK AFTER MACAROON. YOU BE CAREFUL!

YES, WATCH OUT – *HIC!* THAT MALTED WATER IS TREACHEROUS!

SSH! KEEP YOUR VOICE DOWN, MACROBIOTIX!

THE ISLAND WHERE THE CEREMONY WILL TAKE PLACE IS OVER THERE.

FUNNY SORT OF PLACE TO DELIVER MENHIRS!

NESSIE? YOOHOO! ARE YOU THERE?

THE GOURD! NESSIE, THE GOURD! FETCH!

PSCHHHH

MY DOGMATIX FETCHES THINGS TOO.

29A

OH, NO! THAT'S A SET OF BAGPIPES!

EXACTLY AS I FEARED!

SHE UNDERSTANDS, SHE'S DIVING AGAIN!

MY DOGMATIX UNDERSTANDS TOO.

ER... NOT THOSE EITHER, NESSIE. THOSE ARE BROOMS!

ER **?!**

MY DOGMATIX GETS THE IDEA FASTER!

29B

33

FOLLOW ME, OBELIX. I SEE A GALLERY GOING UPWARDS...

THIS ONE MAKES ME LOOK BETTER DRESSED, DON'T YOU THINK?

I HEAR VOICES THAT WAY. LET'S GO AND SEE...

SEVERAL GALLERIES FURTHER ON...

"PORRIDGE AND GRAVY" – I ASK YOU!

AS SOON AS WE GET HERE THEY PUT US ON SENTRY DUTY IN THIS RAT-HOLE!

"LOGISTICAL SUPPORT" MY EYE!

"VERBA VOLANT," AS THEY SAY!

I OUGHT TO HAVE DONE THE SAME AS MY COUSIN LIMITEDNUMBUS WHO'S WORKING ON THE CENSUS IN GAUL. AT LEAST HE'S IN A CUSHY JOB!

31A

SURE ENOUGH, JUST THEN, VERY FAR AWAY...

BOM
BOM
BOM

NO YOU WILL NOT DRAW UP A LIST! NO YOU WILL NOT DRAW UP A LIST!

FULLIAUTOMATIX! STOP BANGING THAT ANVIL AND GO TO BED!

YES, INAUSPICIUS, BUT REMEMBER THAT GAUL ISN'T ALWAYS SIMPLE. THINK OF OUR GARRISON AT TOTORUM!

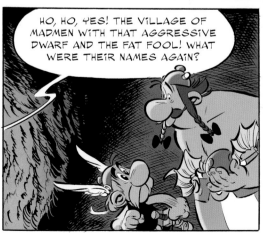

HO, HO, YES! THE VILLAGE OF MADMEN WITH THAT AGGRESSIVE DWARF AND THE FAT FOOL! WHAT WERE THEIR NAMES AGAIN?

?!

ASTERIX AND OBELIX.

BUT HE WASN'T FAT.

31B

WELL, IT ALL STARTED BECAUSE WE WERE LOOKING FOR OYSTERS...

OBELIX, YOU CAN TELL YOUR STORY LATER! WE DON'T WANT TO DAWDLE!

I WENT OVER TO HIM: HE WAS LOOKING AT ME THROUGH THE ICE!

BY TOUTATIS, I COULD HAVE SWORN WE'D BEEN THIS WAY BEFORE!

THEN THE DRUID SAID, "IT'S NOT SERIOUS, HE'S GOT A TUMBLING RUMMY"...

OBELIX, WOULD IT BE TOO MUCH TO ASK YOU TO CONCENTRATE ON THE GALLERY WE'RE LOOKING FOR?

THE GALLERY? BUT WE PASSED IT JUST NOW!

33A

WHAT? AND ONLY NOW YOU TELL US!

I WAS TALKING TO THE FUTURE QUEEN, MISTER ASTERIX!

AND I ADVISE YOU TO CHANGE YOUR TONE, MISTER OBELIX!

THE FUTURE QUEEN AND I DON'T NEED YOUR ADVICE, MISTER ASTERIX! MISTER ASTERIX GIVES TOO MUCH ADVICE ANYWAY!

?

"DON'T SAIL THAT SHIP, DON'T TOSS THAT CABER, DON'T HIT THAT BARD AND GNGNGN AND..."

SHUT UP, OBELIX! THERE'S TOO MUCH OF AN ECHO HERE!

QUICK! LOOK AT THIS! A GALLERY GOING DOWN!

KOF KOF

AND THE DOWNWARD SLOPE BEGINS

GRMBLL AND WHAT'S MORE IF I WANT TO ECHO THEN I WILL ECHO...

OBELIX, YOU'RE GETTING ON MY NERVES!

IT MUST COME OUT ON THE BANK OF THE LOCH!

33B

MEANWHILE... ARE OUR PLANS CLEAR, CENTURION PRETENTIUS?

PERFECTLY CLEAR, O MACVICAR OUR PRIEST! LET ME GO OVER IT ALL AGAIN...

WHEN YOU MAKE YOUR PROCLAMATION, IF SOME OF THE CHIEFTAINS PRESENT DON'T GO ALONG WITH US, OUR LEGIONARIES WILL INTERVENE AND WE'LL TAKE HOSTAGES!

RAPIDITY, EFFICIENCY, SOBRIETY, BY JUPITER!

PERFECT! LET'S DRINK TO THIS NEW COUNTRY THAT WE SHALL BUILD TOGETHER!

TO THE – HIC –
NEW CALEDONIA! AH HA!

BUT NEVER FEAR, ROMANS! **MACCABAEUS REX** WILL NOT BE UNGRATEFUL!

AFTER SWEEPING THROUGH BRITAIN, HE WILL INVITE CAESAR TO **MARCH ON GAUL** WITH HIM!

PFROU!

34A

ER... EXCUSE ME, BUT GAUL ALREADY BELONGS TO US ROMANS...

OR SO TO SPEAK.

OF COURSE, OF COURSE. WE'LL SETTLE ALL THESE LITTLE DETAILS LATER. MORE MALTED WATER?

THANKS – HIC – JUST A DROP!

WE'RE ON DUTY!

DO YOU SEE SOMETHING?

OCH AYE!

HOWEVER HARD I CONCENTRATE, I CAN'T SEE A THING!

OUR POOR COUSINS! SUPPOSE THEY NEVER COME BACK?

34B

DAY IS DAWNING... THE ISLAND IN THE MIDDLE OF THE LOCH IS SEETHING WITH EXCITEMENT BEFORE THE CEREMONY TO ACCLAIM THE NEW KING...

OUIiiinn BOM BOM BOM BOM PEEWIT

BLEEAAT BLEEAAT

...CAUSING CONFUSION AMONG SOME OF THE LOCAL INHABITANTS...

ALL THE LEADING CLAN CHIEFTAINS HAVE COME. PICTS OF THE PLAINS, WOODLAND PICTS, PAUNCHY PICTS, SPOTTED PICTS, LAUGHING PICTS, YELLOW WATER PICTS... YOU COULD CALL THEM A PICKED BUNCH.

OUIiiiiinnn

EVEN A GREAT WHITE PICT HAS COME.

WHITE IS SO ELEGANT!

YES, BUT IT SHOWS THE DIRT.

35A

MACCABAEUS AND HIS SUPPORTERS ADVANCE...

...MINGLING WITH THE CROWD AND BUYING SHOTS OF MALTED WATER TO WIN VOTES...

DRINK TO MACCABAEUS.

MACCABAEUS IS GOOD FOR YOU!

SEE THE CONQUERING HERO COMES!

THE VOTING PROCEDURE FOR A CANDIDATE TO ASCEND THE THRONE IS RATHER COMPLICATED. FIRST COME THE INDEPENDENTS...

YOU KNOW ME, FRIENDS. I DON'T BELONG TO ANY CLAN...

BUT THE ASSEMBLY OF CHIEFTAINS HAS A RIGHT OF VETO.

AND EVEN THE PICT NATS FIND IT HEAVY GOING.

BONK!

35B

AND YOU KNOW ME TOO, FRIENDS! I DON'T JUST TALK OFF THE TOP OF MY HEAD. WITH ME AS YOUR LEADER, WE'LL HAVE A HEAD START!

BONK!

THESE CANDIDATES ARE A REAL HEAD-ACHE!

LET'S HOPE THE NEXT IS BETTER.

TOUCH WOOD!

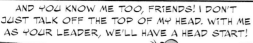

AND NOW MACCABAEUS SPEAKS UP...

YOU REALLY DO KNOW ME, PICTS! YOU KNOW HOW CLOSE I WAS TO OUR DEAR DEPARTED KING, THE GOOD MAC II!

AS PROOF OF HIS TRUST IN ME, DID HE NOT ASK ME TO TAKE CARE OF HIS ADOPTED DAUGHTER, THE ETHEREAL CAMOMILLA?

THAT... HIP-HOP! THAT'S NOT TRUE!

36A

MACAROON?!

MACAROON IS ALIVE?

BUT HE DROWNED... WAS HE FISHED OUT?

HERE'S A FISHY TURN OF EVENTS!

MACAROON? THAT'S IMPOSSIBLE! WHY, I MYSELF... ER, HOW CAN I PUT IT?

PU... PUSHED ME INTO THE LOCH, YOU MEAN?

WELL SAID, SONNY BOY! CARRY ON!

36B

41

42

AND THE ROMANS LAND ON A DISTINCTLY CONFUSED BATTLEFIELD...

ROMAN DISEMBARKMENT

FLOWERED PICT WRESTLING WITH YELLOW WATER PICT

OBELIX CHARGES

ASTERIX BREAKS THROUGH

DRUID SUDDENLY SEES VISION OF NEW GAME

Ziouuu...

OUiiii!!

WHITE PICT INVOKING HIS NEUTRALITY

BARD INSPIRED BY THE BATTLE

BLEEAAT

BLEEAAT

BLEEAAT

REINFORCEMENTS! QUICK! WHY ISN'T THE OTHER BARGE LANDING ITS MEN?

WE WANT TO LAND, BUT THIS THING WON'T LET US!

BROTHERS! STOP THIS POINTLESS QUARRELLING AND LET US UNITE OUR FORCES AGAINST THE ROMAN INVADER!

IT'S NOT FAIR. COME HERE AT ONCE, YOU ROMANS!

MACSTOCK IS RIGHT.

ALL UNITE!

DOWN WITH THE ROMANS!

BUT I TOLD YOU, I'M NEUTRAL!

BLEEAT!

NOTE: THIS WAY OF MOVING OFFICE HEADQUARTERS IS STILL KNOWN AS DELOCHALISATION.

IT IS THOUGHT THAT THE RARITY OVER SEVERAL CENTURIES OF THE CALEDONIAN COCKEREL, A PARTICULARLY SELF-CONSCIOUS FOWL, IS DUE TO THE EXCESSIVE USE OF THIS CRY...

45

AND AFTER A PEACEFUL LITTLE STAY IN THE BOSOM OF THE CLAN...

OUiiiNN... TING TING TING BOM BOM

THANK YOU, MY GAULISH COUSINS. THANKS TO YOU, I AM BACK AT HOME WITH MY OWN PEOPLE, OUR CLANS ARE UNITED, AND ABOVE ALL...

LET'S KEEP IT SHORT! NO SPEECH! COME AND SEE US VERY SOON!

LOOK, OBELIX, I ENGRAVED THE RECIPE FOR YOU...

NICE PEOPLE, THE PICTS, AREN'T THEY, OBELIX?

YES... BUT BETTER NOT BASH THEIR BARDS ALL THE SAME!

GETAFIX WOULD CALL IT CULTURAL DIFFERENCES... HELLO, I THINK WE'RE BEING FOLLOWED!

THE OTTER!

LOOK AT THAT! THE GOURD OF ELIXIR!

BETTER LATE THAN NEVER! THANKS, NESSIE!

TALK ABOUT A MONSTROUS SIZE...

MIGHT AS WELL THROW IT AWAY NOW.

SPLOSH

AND IF, TODAY, CERTAIN DESCENDANTS OF THE ORIGINAL NESSIE ARE SPOTTED DIVING AND COMING UP AGAIN, THEY ARE IN SEARCH OF A LOST GOURD...

LOCH NESS

SOON OUR FRIENDS RETURN IN TRIUMPH TO THEIR VILLAGE.

IMPEDIMENTA! IMPEDIMENTA!

THEY'RE BACK!

46

47

OH, FOR JUPITER'S SAKE! AND NOW WE'LL HAVE TO COUNT THEM ALL AGAIN! HOW IS ANYONE EXPECTED TO TAKE A CENSUS IN A VILLAGE OF MADMEN WHERE THEY KEEP ON MOVING AND DON'T CARE A BIT?

OH YES, I WAS FORGETTING.

PLAF!

AND I DON'T COUNT FOR ANYTHING! I'M SICK OF IT!

WE MUST DO SOMETHING, OBELIX!

WHY NOT SEND HIM TO COUNT THE PICTS?

WE'LL GET A TREE TRUNK, PUT HIM ON IT AND...

HOUUUU...

NO, YOU KNOW DOGMATIX WOULD HATE THAT!

MIGHT AS WELL FINISH IT! REMEMBER, THERE'S A VERY SIMPLE WAY OF COUNTING GAULS!

THERE IS?

OOH, YES! I KNOW WHAT IT IS!

... AND THIS VERY SIMPLE WAY OF COUNTING ALL THE GAULS, NOW REUNITED, AS OUR CLEVER READERS WILL HAVE GUESSED, IS AT **THE GREAT FINAL BANQUET, BY TOUTATIS!**

NOT BAD, HIC! BUT NOT AS GOOD AS BARLEY BEER!

NO, NO, MUCH BIGGER THAN AN OTTER.

AND THEY ALSO RESPECT THEIR BARDS.

THEY DO?

MUNCH MUNCH

XXII XXIII XXIV

THE END

FERRI + CONRAD

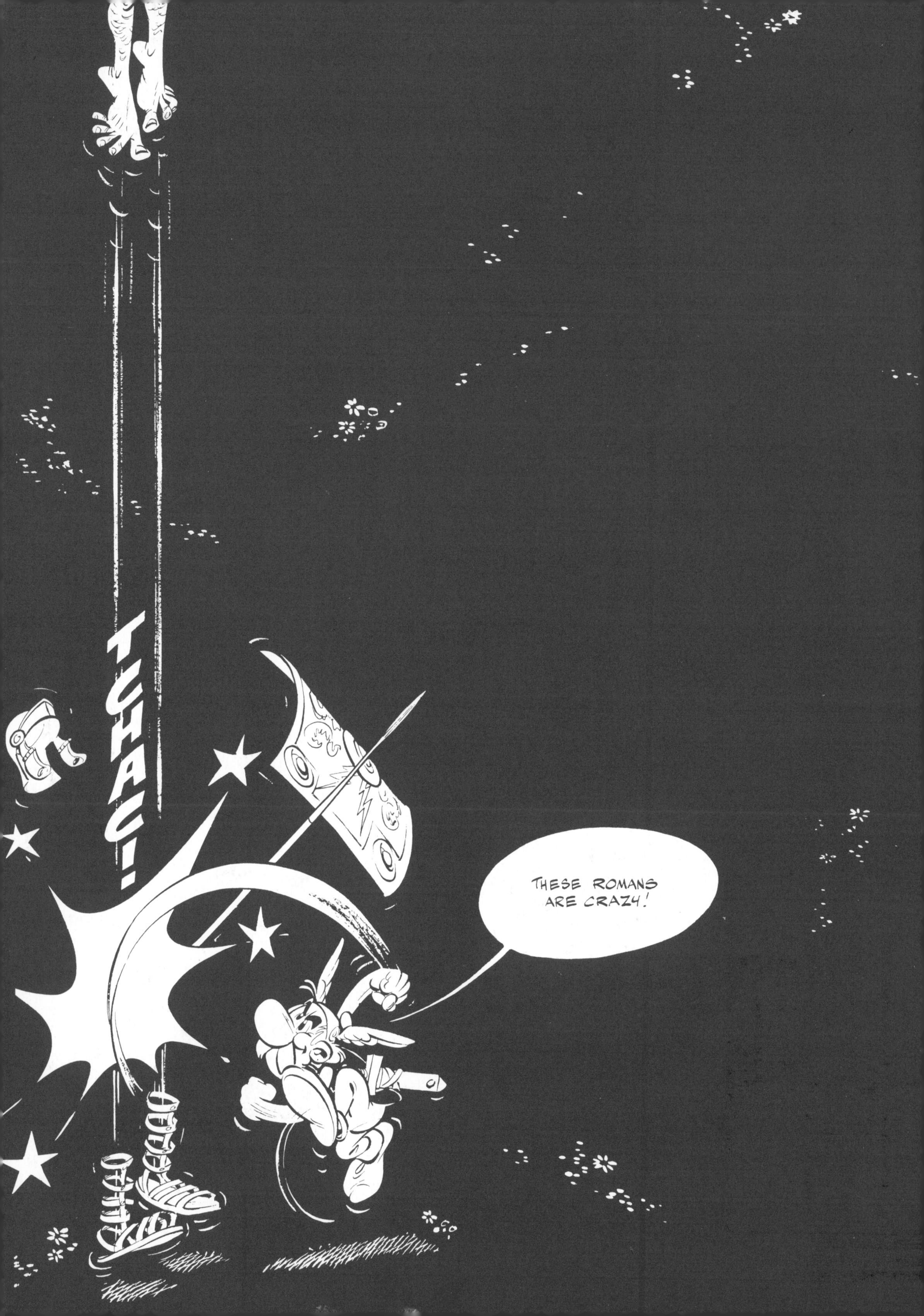
THACK!
THESE ROMANS ARE CRAZY!